Pat Kinevane

Before

GW00541138

methuen | drama

LONDON · NEW YORK · OXFORD · NEW DELHI · SYDNEY

METHUEN DRAMA

Bloomsbury Publishing Plc

50 Bedford Square, London, WC1B 3DP, UK

1385 Broadway, New York, NY 10018, USA

BLOOMSBURY, METHUEN DRAMA and the Methuen Drama logo are
trademarks of Bloomsbury Publishing Plc

First published in Great Britain 2018

Cover design by Drydesign

Photo by Ger Blanch

A catalogue record for this book is available from the British Library.

ISBN: PB: 978-1-3500-9203-7
ePDF: 978-1-3500-9204-4
eBook: 978-1-3500-9205-1

Series: Modern Plays

Typeset by Mark Heslington Ltd, Scarborough, North Yorkshire
Printed and bound in Great Britain

To find out more about our authors and books visit
www.bloomsbury.com and sign up for our *newsletters*.

Fishamble: The New Play Company presents

Before

Written and performed by Pat Kinevane

Directed by Jim Culleton

Composed by Denis Clohessy

Costume Stylist Catherine Condell

Costume Builder Mariad Whisker

Choreographer Emma O'Kane

Music performed by RTÉ Concert Orchestra

Conducted by Cathal Synnott

Graphic Designer Simon Dry

Poster Photography Ger Blanch

Technical Stage Manager Tara Doolan

Stage Manager Ger Blanch

Lighting realised by Tara Doolan based on
concepts by Pat Kinevane and Jim Culleton

Dramaturg Gavin Kostick

Produced by Eva Scanlan

With the voices of Clelia Murphy as the Announcer,
Kez Kinevane as the Guard, and Alex Sharpe as A Stor

The production runs for approximately 80 minutes, with no interval.

About Fishamble: The New Play Company

Fishamble is an Olivier Award-winning, internationally acclaimed Irish theatre company, which discovers, develops and produces new work, across a range of scales. Fishamble is committed to touring throughout Ireland and internationally, and does so through partnerships and collaborations with a large network of venues, festivals and non-arts organisations.

Fishamble has toured its productions to audiences in Ireland as well as to England, Scotland, Wales, France, Germany, Iceland, Croatia, Belgium, Czech Republic, Switzerland, Bulgaria, Romania, Serbia, Turkey, Finland, USA, Canada, New Zealand and Australia.

Fishamble and Pat Kinevane won an Olivier Award for *Silent* in 2016, when it was presented at Soho Theatre. Other awards for Fishamble productions include Scotsman Fringe First, Herald Angel, Argus Angel, 1st Irish, The Stage, Adelaide Fringe Best Theatre, Dublin Fringe, EMA, In Dublin, Forbes' Best Theater, Stage Raw LA, and Irish Times Theatre awards, as well as Writers Guild of Ireland/ZeBBie and Stewart Parker Trust awards for many of its playwrights. Fishamble's living archive is in the National Library of Ireland.

Fishamble is at the heart of new writing for theatre in Ireland, not just through its productions, but through its extensive programme of Training, Development and Mentoring schemes. These currently include *A Play for Ireland,* the *New Play Clinic* and *Show in a Bag*, which is run in partnership with Dublin Fringe Festival and Irish Theatre Institute. Each year, Fishamble typically supports 60% of the writers of all new plays produced on the island of Ireland, approximately 55 plays per year.

'Fishamble puts electricity in the National Grid of Dreams'
Sebastian Barry

'a global brand with international theatrical presence'
Irish Times

'Ireland's leading new writing company' The Stage

'forward-thinking Fishamble' New York Times

'excellent Fishamble … Ireland's terrific Fishamble' Guardian

Fishamble's recent and current productions include:

- *Before* by Pat Kinevane in association with the Strollers Network (2018)

- *Rathmines Road* by Deirdre Kinahan in coproduction with the Abbey Theatre (2018)

- *Drip Feed* by Karen Cogan in coproduction with Soho Theatre (2018)

- *GPO 1818* by Colin Murphy to mark the bicentenary of the GPO (2018)

- *Haughey|Gregory* by Colin Murphy in the Abbey Theatre, Mountjoy Prison, Dáil Éireann, and Croke Park (2018)

- *Maz & Bricks* by Eva O'Connor on national and international tour (2017–18)

- *Forgotten*, *Silent* and *Underneath* by Pat Kinevane (since 2007, 2011 and 2014, respectively – 2018) touring in Ireland, UK, Europe, US, Australia and New Zealand

- *On Blueberry Hill* by Sebastian Barry on national and international tour (2017)

- *The Humours of Bandon* by Margaret McAuliffe (2017–18) on national and international tour

- *Charolais* by Noni Stapleton (2017) in New York

- *Inside the GPO* by Colin Murphy (2016) performed in the GPO during Easter

- *Tiny Plays for Ireland and America* by 26 writers (2016) at the Kennedy Center, Washington DC, and Irish Arts Center, New York, as part of *Ireland 100*

- *Mainstream* by Rosaleen McDonagh (2016) in coproduction with Project Arts Centre

- *Invitation to a Journey* by David Bolger, Deirdre Gribbin and Gavin Kostick (2016) in coproduction with CoisCeim, Crash Ensemble and Galway International Arts Festival

- *Little Thing, Big Thing* by Donal O'Kelly (2014–16) touring in Ireland, UK, Europe, US and Australia

- *Swing* by Steve Blount, Peter Daly, Gavin Kostick and Janet Moran (2014–16) touring in Ireland, UK, Europe, US, Australia and New Zealand

- *Spinning* by Deirdre Kinahan (2014) at Dublin Theatre Festival

- *The Wheelchair on My Face* by Sonya Kelly (2013–14) touring in Ireland, UK, Europe and US

Fishamble Staff: Jim Culleton (Artistic Director), Eva Scanlan (General Manager), Gavin Kostick (Literary Manager), Chandrika Narayanan-Mohan (Marketing and Fundraising Executive), Ronan Carey (Office and Production Coordinator)

Fishamble Board: Tania Banotti, Padraig Burns, Elizabeth Davis, Peter Finnegan, Doireann Ní Bhriain, Vincent O'Doherty, John O'Donnell, Siobhan O'Leary, Andrew Parkes (Chair)

About Fishamble and Pat Kinevane

Fishamble produced Pat's first play *The Nun's Wood* in 1998, followed by his second play *The Plains of Enna* in 1999. Fishamble is very proud to have commissioned, developed and produced three solo plays written and performed by Pat, which continue to tour extensively. They are *Forgotten* (since 2006), *Silent* (since 2011) and *Underneath* (since 2014), all directed by Jim Culleton. The plays have been performed in over 60 venues throughout Ireland, and are all published by Bloomsbury Methuen Drama. *Silent* has won Olivier, Fringe First, Herald Angel and Argus Angel awards, and *Underneath* won Fringe First, LA Stage Raw and Adelaide Fringe Best Theatre awards, and was nominated for Offie/Off West End and Total Theatre awards. The productions have toured throughout Europe, with partners including Dance Base (Edinburgh), Soho Theatre (London), CCI (Paris), Prague Fringe Festival, Lokal Festival (Reykjavik), International Theatre Festival (Sibiu), Tron Theatre (Glasgow), Cymru Theatr Clwyd, Irish Festival (Oulu), GLAS (Geneva), Home (Manchester), INFANT Festival (Novi Sad), Brighton Festival, Hotbed Festival (Cambridge), nu:write (Zagreb), and to Leuven, Kaiserslautern, Trabzon, and all across Bulgaria. In the US, in association with Georganne Aldrich Heller, they were presented by the Irish Arts Center, New York, Boston Center for the Arts, Source Theatre in Washington D.C. and the Odyssey Theatre in Los Angeles. In Australia, *Silent* toured with Arts Projects Australia to Perth and Melbourne, and *Underneath* toured to Adelaide.

Development of *Before*

Before was commissioned by Fishamble and has been in development during 2017–18, with the support of the Arts Council, National Theatre Studio (London), Georganne Aldrich Heller, Robert Leroy, RTE Concert Orchestra and Pavilion Theatre. The development process was supported by an award from the Stroller's Touring Network.

Fishamble wishes to thank the following Friends of Fishamble & Corporate Members for their invaluable support:

Alan & Rosemary Ashe, ATM Accounting Services, Mary Banotti, Tania Banotti, Doireann Ní Bhriain, Conor Braiden, Business to Arts, Breda Cashe, Maura Connolly, John & Yvonne Healy, Gillie Hinds, Monica McInerney, Stuart Mclaughlin, Ger McNaughton, Sinead Moriarty, Pat Moylan, Dympna Murray, Lisney, Liz Nugent, Vincent O'Doherty, Nora Owen, David & Veronica Rowe, Mary Stephenson, Patrick Sutton, and Tesco Finest. Thank you also to all those who do not wish to be credited.

fishamble.com   facebook.com/fishamble   twitter.com/fishamble

Fishamble is funded by The Arts Council and Dublin City Council. Its international touring is supported by Culture Ireland.

Acknowledgements

Thanks to the following for their help with this production: Rachel West and all at the Arts Council; Ray Yeates and all at Dublin City Council Arts Office; all 10 venues in the Stroller's Touring Network; Laura MacNaughton, Aoife McCollum and all at the O'Reilly Theatre; all at 3 Great Denmark Street; Nina Steiger and all at the National Theatre Studio; Ruth Little; Georganne Aldrich Heller; Robert Leroy; Hugh Murray and all at Pavilion Theatre; Mary Sexton, Gareth Hudson, Mary Adams, Andrew Smith and all at RTÉ Concert Orchestra; Laura and all those who have helped since this publication went to print.

Biographies

Pat Kinevane is a native of Cobh, Co. Cork. He has worked as an actor in theatre, film, television and radio for 29 years. In 2016, Pat won an Olivier Award in London for his Outstanding Achievement as an Actor and a Writer that year. This prestigious award was shared with Fishamble and Jim Culleton who have been integral to the production and direction of Pat's three solo shows. As a writer, he completed his first full-length play *The Nun's Wood* in 1997, which won a BBC Stewart Parker Trust Award and was produced by Fishamble. Fishamble then produced his second play *The Plains of Enna* (Dublin Theatre Festival 1999). Pat wrote *The Death of Herod* for *Mysteries 2000* at the SFX. In 2008 his piece *Evangeline Elsewhere* premiered in New York in the First Irish Festival.

Pat has been touring since 2006 with his three solo pieces, *Forgotten* (Irish Times Theatre Award Nominee), *Silent* (Scotsman Fringe First, Herald Angel and Brighton Argus Angel Award) and *Underneath* (Scotsman Fringe First and Adelaide Fringe Awards) all produced by Fishamble.

Pat is deeply thankful to Fishamble for all of their work and endless support.

Jim Culleton is the artistic director of Fishamble: The New Play Company. For Fishamble, he has directed productions which have toured throughout Ireland, UK, Europe, Australia, New Zealand, Canada and the US. Jim previously directed Pat Kinevane's other solo plays *Forgotten*, *Silent* and *Underneath*, which have toured to 60 Irish venues and 17 other countries. His productions for Fishamble have won over a dozen Irish and international awards, including an Olivier Award for *Silent*. He has also directed for companies including the Abbey Theatre, Woodpecker/the Gaiety, 7:84 (Scotland), Project Arts Centre, Amharclann de hIde, Tinderbox, The Passion Machine, The Ark, Second Age, RTE Radio 1, The Belgrade, TNL Canada, Dundee Rep Ensemble, Draíocht, Barnstorm, TCD School of Drama, Frontline Defenders, CoisCéim/Crash Ensemble/GIAF, RTE lyric fm, Origin (New York), Vessel (Australia), and Symphony Space Broadway/Irish Arts Center (New York). Jim has taught for NYU, NUIM, GSA, Uversity, the Lir, Notre Dame, Villanova, TCD and UCD. For Fishamble, he most recently directed *Rathmines Road* by Deirdre Kinahan (Abbey Theatre co-production) and will next direct *On Blueberry Hill* by Sebastian Barry in New York and on national tour.

Denis Clohessy has previously worked with Fishamble, including the productions *On Blueberry Hill*, *The Pride of Parnell Street*, *Silent*, *Underneath*, *Spinning*, *Mainstream* and *Strandline.* He has also produced work for theatre and dance with The Abbey Theatre, The Gate Theatre, Rough Magic, Corn Exchange, Junk Ensemble and many others. He won the Irish Times Theatre Award for Best Design Sound in 2011 for Rough Magic's *Sodome, My Love*, he was a nominee in 2015 (for Junk Ensemble's *It Folds*), was an associate artist with the Abbey in 2008 and was a participant on Rough Magic's ADVANCE programme in 2012. His work in film and television includes the films *Older than Ireland* (Snack Box Films), *The Irish Pub* (Atom Films), *His and Hers* (Venom Film), *The Land of the Enlightened* (Savage Film), *In View* (Underground Cinema), *The Reluctant Revolutionary* (Underground Films) and the television series *Limits of Liberty* (South Wind Blows) performed by the RTE Concert Orchestra.

Catherine Condell recently worked on *Silent* and *Underneath* by Pat Kinevane for Fishamble: The New Play Company, and *Payback!* by Maria McDermottroe and Marion O'Dwyer as part of *Show in a Bag*. Catherine has worked in the fashion industry for 35 years, initially as a display artist and then as fashion stylist and fashion show producer. She worked for the Brown Thomas group for over 20 years and produced the Supermodel Shows in 1996, 2000 & 2003. She has worked with Naomi Campbell, Christy Turlington, Helena Christensen, Yasmin Le Bon, Eva Herzigova and Erin O'Connor.

Emma O'Kane is a freelance dance artist and choreographer. She trained at the Perm State Choreographic Academy, Russia. She previously worked with Fishamble and Pat Kinevane on *Underneath*. Choreographic credits include *A Portrait of the Artist as a Young Man* (Rough Magic), *160 Voices* (a commission by GPO Public Art & Dublin Dance Festival), *The Chilean Trilogy* (Prime Cut Productions), *Silent Moves* by Aideen Barry (Ignite! Mayo) winner of Modern Ireland in 100 Artworks 2015, *Jockey*, *BEES!*, *Farm* and *CARE (*Willfredd Theatre) *Angel Meadow*, *Laundry*, *Basin* (Anu Productions), *The Ballet Ruse* (co-created with Muirne Bloomer). She has been a member of CoisCéim Dance Theatre since 2001. Dance Europe voted Emma Outstanding Dancer of the Year for her performance in CoisCéim's production of *FAUN*. Recent performance credits include *These Rooms* (Anu/CoisCéim) at LIFT & 14–18 NOW. Emma has an MA in Dance from the University of Limerick.

Clelia Murphy is familiar to many for her long-running role of Niamh Brennan in RTÉ's flagship drama series *Fair City*. She most recently filmed the role of Kathleen Buckley in feature film *Danny Boy* directed by Ferdia Mac Anna. Other recent roles include Rhiannon in Bernard Dunne's *Mythical Creatures* and Lorraine in Deadpan Picture's new comedy series for RTÉ 2, *Nowhere Fast*, created by Alison Spittle. On stage, Clelia most recently played the role of Maeve in a touring production of *Boom* by Isobel Mahon, directed by Caroline FitzGerald. Other recent theatre credits include the role of Lulubelle LaVelle in John Murphy's touring musical *Elvis is My Daddy* and the role of Frau Gabor in *Spring Awakening*, directed by the internationally acclaimed György Vidovszy. Film credits include Vivienne de Courcy's feature *Dare to be Wild*, Jack Conroy's *The Gaelic Curse*, *JFK.The Badgeman Conspiracy* directed by John Sheridan and Paul Valentine and the short film *Clean Slate* directed by Will Morgan for Wytao Films. Clelia also worked on *Grabbers* for Samson Films, Parallel Pictures' *The Gift of the Magi*, and Stephen Kane's award-winning *The Crooked Mile*. In 2015, Clelia co-produced and starred in Jennifer Davidson's award-winning short *Waiting For Tom*, directed by Ruth O'Looney, which was officially selected to screen at the Galway Film Fleadh, Cork, Foyle, Dingle and Chicago film festivals. It also screened in the Irish Film Festival London where it won Best Short. Clelia is also one of Ireland's most experienced VO artists with a career that has seen her lending her voice to some of Ireland's biggest brands and best-loved shows. Radio work includes working with John Boorman on his radio play *The Hitlist*, Bill Hughes' *Grace*, Joe O'Byrne's *Crane* and Catherine Brennan's *The Guilty Heart*. In 2017 she voiced the role of Miss Higgins in *Kinsey One Through Five* by Veronica Coburn, produced by Kevin Reynolds for RTÉ Radio Drama on One. Clelia trained with the Gaiety School of Acting, was a member of Dublin Youth Theatre and also holds an MA in screenwriting.

Introducing orchestral music to new audiences since 1948, the **RTÉ Concert Orchestra** has built a strong connection with the public that saw it named the World's Favourite Orchestra 2015, winning 25% of the vote in an international poll. The orchestra is committed to an eclectic range of programming across various genres, meaning that no two RTÉ CO audiences are ever the same. It is as likely to be found presenting the world premiere of *Mise Éire* with live performance of Ó Riada's score in the presence of the President Michael D. Higgins (2016) as performing live at Electric Picnic with RTÉ 2fm's Jenny

Greene (2017) or recording a one-off TV special with Niall Horan (2018).

RTÉ CO has performed with countless extraordinary artists across all genres. From the classical world, Pavarotti, Domingo, Carreras and Lang Lang; film and stage composers including Lalo Schifrin, Michel Legrand, David Arnold and Marvin Hamlisch; stars of jazz and musical theatre like Michael Feinstein, Cleo Laine and Kurt Elling. Even a quick roll call of the orchestra's collaborations with Irish artists gives a flavour of the range and calibre: Colm Wilkinson, Sharon Shannon, Duke Special, Declan O'Rourke, The Coronas, Horslips, Sinéad O'Connor, Imelda May and Lúnasa.

Cathal Synnott studied at The Schola Cantorum at St Finian's College, Mullingar and subsequently at Trinity College, Dublin. Since then he has flourished as one of the theatre and music industry's most respected musical directors. Highly acclaimed for his precision and musicianship, his work as musical director/musician includes: *Riverdance* (Broadway and International tours), *Blind Fiddler* (Lyric Theatre Belfast, 2002) *Improbable Frequency* (Rough Magic, 2003), *Sweeney Todd* (Gate Theatre, 2007), *Flatpack* (Ulysses Opera Co., 2012), *Anglo the Musical* (Verdant Productions, 2012), *Threepenny Opera* (Gate Theatre, 2013) *Into the Woods* (Lir Academy, 2014) *The Train* (Rough Magic, 2015/2017) *The Cradle Will Rock* (Lir Academy, 2015), *Christmas with the Priests* (Irish Tour, 2015), *Once* (Landmark Productions, 2016), *Town is Dead* (Abbey Theatre, 2016), *Anna Karenina* (Abbey Theatre, 2016), *Jacques Brel is Alive and Well and Living in Paris* (Gate Theatre, 2017), *Camille O'Sullivan – The Carny Dream* (Bound & Gagged, 2017), *Assassins* (Gate Theatre, 2018), *Copperface Jacks – The Musical* (Verdant Productions, 2018).

Alex Sharpe's career spans a rich variety of experience as an actress and singer throughout Ireland, Europe and the United States. She started her professional career as 'Dorothy' in the Olympia's production of *The Wizard of Oz* which led to multiple lead roles in musical theatre and pantomime on the stages of Ireland's foremost theatres. She toured the UK playing 'Eponine' in Cameron Mackintosh's production of *Les Miserables* alongside Colm Wilkinson. She originated the role of 'Bernadette' in Andrew Lloyd Webber's world premiere of *The Beautiful Game* at the Cambridge Theatre, London. As a singer, Alex has appeared extensively as guest soloist with the RTÉ Concert Orchestra, the BBC Philharmonic, the Halle, Birmingham City Orchestra and the Mormon Tabernacle Choir and

Orchestra, to name but a few. Alex is best known in the United States as a former member of the group Celtic Woman. She is currently a member and the founder of the musical group CaraNua.

Gavin Kostick, as Literary Manager at Fishamble, works with new writers for theatre through script development, readings and a variety of mentorship programmes. For Fishamble Gavin is particularly proud of his work on *Show in a Bag*, *The New Play Clinic*, *Tiny Plays for Ireland* and *A Play for Ireland*. Gavin is also an award-winning playwright. He has written over twenty plays which have been produced nationally and internationally. Recent favourite works include *Invitation to a Journey* and *The End of the Road*, *This is What we Sang* for Kabosh, *Fight Night*, *The Games People Play* and *At the Ford* for RISE and the Libretto for *The Alma Fetish* for Raymond Deane and Wide Open Opera. As a performer he performed Joseph Conrad's *Heart of Darkness: Complete*, a six-hour show for Absolut Fringe, Dublin Theatre Festival and The London Festival of Literature at the Southbank. His work in all areas has received many national and international awards.

Eva Scanlan is the General Manager and Producer of Fishamble: The New Play Company. Current and recent producing work includes *On Blueberry Hill* by Sebastian Barry, Fishamble's award-winning Pat Kinevane Trilogy on tour in Ireland and internationally, *The Humours of Bandon* by Margaret McAuliffe, *Maz and Bricks* by Eva O'Connor, *Inside the GPO* by Colin Murphy, *Tiny Plays for Ireland and America* at the Kennedy Center in Washington DC and the Irish Arts Center in New York, and *Swing* by Steve Blount, Peter Daly, Gavin Kostick and Janet Moran on tour in Ireland, the UK, and Australia. Eva produces *The 24 Hour Plays: Dublin* at the Abbey Theatre in Ireland (2012-present), in association with The 24 Hour Play Company, New York, and has worked on The 24 Hour Plays on Broadway and The 24 Hour Musicals at the Gramercy Theatre. Previously, she was Producer of terraNOVA Collective in New York (2012–2015), where she produced *terraNOVA Rx: Four Plays in Rep* at IRT Theater, the soloNOVA Arts Festival, the Groundworks New Play Series, *Woman of Leisure and Panic* (FringeNYC), *P.S. Jones and the Frozen City*, among other projects.

Before

A Play with Much Music

For my bravest buddy Brian Roche
&
In Loving Memory of the most beautiful Siobhan Miley

AUTHOR'S NOTE

On a riverside walk beside the Boyne, I met a dead Mink. A beautifully formed jet creature just lying on lush grass. I got very upset at the thought of its young life being brutally over. I had met Minks and Stoats before but this one was only a child. I thought of its parents. Would they know of its death? If so, would they grieve? Would they blame themselves . . . or each other for not teaching it to be safe around passing cars, humans or hawks? Would either of them skin the child and wear its fur over their own adult hide to gloat that they were the better parent and had the monopoly on that role? Good Jesus . . . that's what went through my churning mind on the banks of that stream – a body of water once red with the corpuscles of Battle.

And the battles continue daily all across Éire. Sons alienated from their Fathers, Daughters kept away from Mothers... all because one parent believes that they are the better or the more righteous guardian. Some are indeed valid wars, especially when admirably protecting a child from harm or neglect. But other battles are not so noble . . . parents swinging at each other with insults, accusations and animalistic hatred. But the biggest weapon they use is the child that they once shared. They viciously injure each other, but are damaging that child for its entire life in the process. For any parent to deny their child its other parent because of grudge or petty anger . . . they may as well skin that beautifully formed creature and wear it over their own selfish pelt . . . A Mink . . . to gloat of their own parental Victory.

Eva, Gavin, Ronan and Chandrika at Fishamble have been extraordinary to work with over the last 13 years. They have nurtured and protected me, constantly. Working again this time with Denis Clohessy was a huge privilege and joy. He is a magnificent composer. Jim Culleton has a serene energy which bathes and swathes every word of a script. He cares deeply for the intent, thoughts and efforts of the writer. He is gifted to deal with my ups and downs and madness. He is a beautifully patient and creative director devoid of ego and negativity. I have felt safe to fly to the crazy places in my world with him by my side as a writer and performer. He takes my fear away and reminds me of my playfulness and glee. He is a consummate professional and stunning creator of theatrical event. I would have stopped both writing and acting years ago if it were not for his compassion and belief in me.

I am overwhelmed with gratitude to anyone who ever helped or encouraged me to do my work. I am forever thankful. All my Love,

Pat Kinevane 2018

AUTHOR'S THANKS

My Mother, Marie, My Late Father Denis and Brother Alan, My Sisters, Betty and Julie, My Brothers, John, Denis and Mattie, My Late Aunt, Teresa O Rourke, and all of my extended family. Big thanks and huge love to Fionnuala Murphy, Kez Kinevane, Claudia Carroll, Frank Mackey, Fiona Lalor, Marion O'Dwyer, Catherine Condell, Ger Blanch, Denis Clohessy, Clodagh O'Donoghue, Amelia Crowley, Anthony Brophy, Anne Layde, Claire Cullinane (RIP and I will always love you Claire), Noreen Brennan, Clelia Murphy, Conor and Maria McDermottroe, Fiona Condon, Lt. Comm Liam Smith (RIP), Joan O Hara (RIP), Des Cave, John Olohan, Maire Hastings and Andy O Ghallichor (RIP), Helen Norton, Marion Mc Auliffe, Siobhan Miley (RIP), Georganne Aldrich Heller and Robert Leroy, Noelle Brown, Olwen Fouere, Rachael Rogers, Sinead Keenan and Stefan Buttner, Niall Toner, Caitriona Ni Mhurchu, Liza Moynihan, Dessie Gallagher, Malachy McKenna, Brian Roche, Fergal Murphy, David Swartz, and all of dearest friends for their constant care and support. I love you all so very much.

A Blank Black Box of a Beautiful Stage.

Black Flowing Fringing hangs near the back wall.

A Black Chair and Table downstage left.

The Announcements are from an innocent yet sumptuous Mother-Ireland.

The Guard is a rough Jackeen-Howya.

Aster sounds of Angelic Champs Elysee.

Bees, Flash, Thunder, Flames, Dunk, Catscream, Cows etc . . . are Ultra Close Events for the Ears.

Houselights fade to black as the Overture begins . . . Cellos and Violas and a melodic vocal Ahh Ahh Ahh x 12 followed by a close voiceover of '5 o'clock this morning. The blackbirds called the Sun. It shot up over Lamont. I got all the milkin done. For I'm Travellin up, travellin up to Dublin'. Then Enormous Thunder . . . then sounds of very heavy rain pour into the space and are interrupted by an alarm clock, silence, then a Dawning chorus of cows, birds, more cows, a dog, birds, whistle, cows, gate, cows, birds, the dog, cows, dog, cows loud, water, cows, water, dog, birds, razor shower, dog, cows, car, dog, beep, car distant, a bus, traffic, seagulls, beeps, pulse, beeps, blood pulse, water, traffic, blood pulsing in valves, lights, a silhouette, vague and voiceover . . . music beneath in the vicinity of an overture distant but beautiful . . . A man . . . Pontius . . . appears in lowest light . . . His Silhouette dances his journey through the street. We hear his recorded voice as we are inside his head . . .

Pontius   That must be the spike, the stiletto in the Ghetto . . . It's shit!! That's why she didn't want to meet under it I suppose. That's what she said on the second page of the letter. 'What a wasted opportunity,' she said. If it had a stairs inside it itself ye could climb up an gander something stunnin from on high whoooooo, that was close Jesus the Luas and the GPO. God bless the women and men who fought.

Sudden heavy Rain and instinctive brolly up.

Fuckin downpour. Hope the cattle are under the hedge now.
I'll be home soon girls to milk ye again under the Rainbow I
promise. Relax. Now lad, nearly there. Here we go . . . our
version of Harrods. The store that has it all . . .

Guard   Welcome to Clery's Sir.

Pontius   Where the fuck did that come out of?

Guard   Pissin down in the middle of June!

Pontius (*shaking brolly*)   Just up for the day.

Guard   Hang up yer coat ya mad spanner! It'll dry
while ya shop.

As he unties his trenchcoat and we suspend time . . .

Pontius   How's it goin? Me nerves is in bits!!! I'm gonna
meet me Daughter. She's 21 today. You are the first people
to ever know that!

*During the following female voiceover, he hands the coat and brolly
to the Guard and dumbshows a chat as he fixes his clothing . . .*

Announcement 1 (*bing bong*)   Customers welcome to Clery's
Department Store on this June 12 2015 and it's good to be
seen in our Millinery section today because we have mid-
season madness for all you city and country ladies who are
getting ready for a wedding or the horses or if you simply
would like to wear something pretty up on your head!

Number Hats 1

I think I've seen all this before
It must be happening again
I'm floating like I've lost an Oar
A million seconds feel like ten

It's very familiar and for the first time
It's over similar but that's the trick of the mind
Cos my head must be cheating this crazy repeating
I think I've seen all this before

The story is starting once more
The dawn and the bus and the day shaa vuuus
The moment I came through the door
The faces and smiles and the how are yous

My Mama used to sing
Oh how did it go?
She'd travel up to Dublin
In thunder and snow
Up from the Country
For ribbons and bows
For every occasion
Oh how did it go
You can't bate Clery's for a classy Chapeau
You can't bate Clery's for a classy Chapeau

Who the fuck uses a word like Chapeau?
It's not like she was French or German
She hadn't a note in her beautiful head
No Julie Andrews or Ethel Merman
But she loved Vaudeville and operettas too
A star she was born with satin and glitter and glue
They'd ask for one costume she'd make them thirty-two
One for each county in Eire!

(*Spoken, smiling*)   Where did that come out of!!? I've never told this to anybody in my life . . . nobody knows . . . all the details and the gore. But I am free now, so here goes. Firstly, I always fuckin hated Musicals!!

CAR CRASH . . . followed by underscore of growing grandeur . . .

Dada was the only Postman in Lamont and painted all the scenery for the local musical society. They called him Maurice Minor cos he was the head off that French actor Maurice Chevalier but just 5ft nothin and a snout like the Concorde!! And he hated being on stage . . . wud shit himself . . . but was in huge demand to do Ghost Singing from behind a screen with a microphone. Magnificent voice . . . like a Chocolate Symphony. They put the juvenile lead out front just mouthing away to South Pacific or Carousel and Dada givin it socks behind him. He gave Mama a different fresh flower for her hair every day and she gorgeous and gifted making costumes. She would transform a grubby bedspread into a gown from Versailles in the length of a hurling match using odds n ends and allsorts of feckulata. I recall her making 20 kimonos from paper potato bags all painted by hand for the Mikado. She even got Dada to stand in and fill out the chorus and he did because he fucking adored her and I knew he was so nervous cos the sweat was seeping through his Japanese back so he kept sneaking snips of poteen from his flask. Shur that flask was his Samurai sword for each passing day. Ould Pet. Ould fool! Maurice Minor . . . The singing Fool!

FLAMES . . .

Announcement 2 (*bing bong with some distant music beneath*) This Iconic shop is 160 years old and was once called 'The Palatial Mart'! We used to have a ballroom on the upper floor with a full Orchestra seven nights a week. That didn't last . . . but we have survived 2 full world wars and bankruptcies galore!! Clery's is still here, from fashions to furniture . . . for everything and anyone you want to buy for . . .

Pontius   Some folk are impossible to buy for. Mama said it's because they are usually the ones who are impossible to know . . . that they are the secret keepers and the wise of the world. She was mostly afloat herself like that . . . frequently staring up to the sky, or the Welkin as she would call it . . . smilin at spirits and premonitions from elsewhere. She told me, when I was 6, that there was no such thing as Time! Just now . . . and that Clocks were made to put order on memories and to harness the chaos of whatever lay ahead . . . that us humans invented Time to make sense of the Sun and the Moon, but that beyond the Welkin was Forever, and not a trace of Time. Her grandmother was a healer quack from Mayo! Anyway, I'm early today and I am shopping for

me daughter. Her name is Aster. I calls her A Stor . . . My
love . . . my Dear . . . and it is hard to know what to buy her
and I meetin her in an hour and I haven't seen her since she
was 4 years old . . . exactly 17 year ago.

BEES . . .

Hats 2

It's high definition from mountains away
It's my recollection but like the first day
The tellers are cashing the pictures are flashing
I know I've seen all this before

I'm certain I heard this before
The Girly voice on the microphone
It isn't sharp, it isn't sore
But fuzzy and warm like a twilight zone

My Mama sang a song
Excited I suppose
And planning her outfits
From eyebrows to toes
For every production
For fabrics galore
For all celebrations
Oh how did it go?
From the bridges of Derry to the gap of Dunloe
Ya can't bate Clery's for a wedding or a show
Ya can't top Clery's for a Belle or a Beau
Ya can't bate Clery's for a classy Chapeau
Ya can't bate Clery's for a classy Chapeau.

FLASH . . .

(*Spoken*) So there was Mama and Dada and Mercia and Me
h-a-p-p-y happy. They dipped me into a Belfast sink on the
21st March 1965 because they thought I was dying from a
whooping cough at only 2 weeks old and the priest was
snowbound and they gave me the name of Pontius. Now let's
clear the air and say yes after the Pilot fella and Mama was

never a church goer but she loved her Bible and promised to
call my sister Mercia after all those who have been
compassionate and me after the Governor of Judea as she
always admired him for washing his hands of the sentencing
of the Christ named Jesus in the year 33.

Dunk . . .

Some fuckers never wash their hands! I sees it all the time in
the men's toilet. Dirty bastards after handlin their mickeys or
wiping their arses and they just fix the belt or the tie and
then straight past the basin out the door spreading germs!!!
Does that happen in the women's??! Dirty fuckers . . . Takin
a chance . . . Just gettin away with it!!!

Announcement 3 (*bing bong*)   Customers – the sizzling value
today would put a body in mind of the great Rising of 1916
when it was so battlehot in Clery's that even the very glass in
the display windows melted!! And again today we are
combusting our prices in Lingerie! Fancy a change of
knickers or bra? Then rush to Ladies Underwear and you
won't believe your thighs!!!

Number Lingerie 1

I know and I always knew and most of you know it too
That anything can happen in a musical
I know it's ridiculous I feel like a dick because
The strangest shit will pop up in a musical
I always hated watching them cos most of the plots
Would start off quite believable and join all the dots
Then suddenly the characters get tied into knots
And fuck themselves off balconies in musicals!

For Example . . .

She's a nanny in Siam he's a king baldy bastard he can't sing
She's a Sandy virgin he's a jock durin summer lovin she gets cock
He's Rich with a flock of children and she's a nun up a Nazi
mountain on the run
He's a phantom minger – she's a ride a singer . . . Andrew Webber
what a fuckin winner

No matter how you try to forget the fact there's always gonna be
backing track to life just like there is in fucking musicals !

(*Spoken*) Mama quotes Matthew 10.6 'Be as wise as serpents
and gentle as doves' I remember seein her with her best
friend who lived next door . . . The Pelican Plunket. I was
only 5 but never forget them clung to each other and
vomiting tears and the Pelican left the town and Mama was
really quiet until she came back a year later and they
vomiting cries again for days. The Pelican never married but
was the sister Mama never had. Beautiful Mama. How I
loved ya how I loved ya . . . And my Angel Sister Mercia.
D'you know Vivien Leigh? The spit o' her, pocket size
version, and would always be 'well fiddledy diddley diddley
dee'. To lose people 'that' near to you, is when ye realise that
being alive is an agony as well as a bliss. The Brutality of
Subtraction. But to lose someone and they still alive is
sometimes worse than if they fully died. The longin to see
them never goes. The vicious Ache of missin them. Some
folk get over loss. Some never recover . . . Because of the
hell, the inferno of Pain.

CAT SCREAM . . .

Lingerie 2

It's perfectly natural in the middle of disaster just to
burst out into harmony in musicals (musicals)
When feeling les Myserable it's always Advyasble
to tap away your troubles in a musical
There's no, There's no, There's no . . .

Announcement 4 (*bing bong*)   There's no end to the
tempting cakes in our Clery's Café t'day ! Ladies . . . pretend
you are in Venice with a cuppa and a muffin . . . and we
know that you gentlemen prefer scones!!!

There's one about some prisoners in knickers and bras
There's one about a bang bang and shitty ould cars
There's one about these pussycats at midnight in bars

Touccccccchchhchh Meeeeeeee!!!!!! . . . . . .
Cos any shite is possble in a musical

She's Puerto Rico Maria he's a Jet stabs a Shark double death
Evita Peron in her big blonde bun waving like that to Argentina.
She's a Guy and he's a Doll both are played by Jerry Hall
Miss Saigon is really the Slicker, but did ya know in Lamont it's
the name of the local Chipper!
So from the Cliffs of Moher to Arkansas there's always gonna be
an orchestra behind you like there is in fucking musicals

Spoken as if relaxing with tea in Italy!

Mammy quoting Ecclesiasticus 'Whatever thy hand findeth
to do, do it with all thy might.' Did ya ever think to yourself,
Jesus, this could be the very last time I will ever do this? Be it
stirring this cuppa or cutting your toenails or shaving yer
jaw or yawning like a hippo or laughing out loud or
swallowing cake or kissin wet lips or gazing into your own
deep eyes in the bathroom mirror. Well I thought that on
the way up here. Makes me relish the day even more for how
special it all is going to be. For her, and me. The first time,
and the last time this will ever happen.

Sings . . . . . . softly and warmly in mock tragedy

Lingerie 3

I was always a crow so I really don't know
Why I'm crooning here now like a jerk
As a boy I would curse as I heard them rehearse
Down the back of the hall doin homework

But the lyric osmosis it must have seeped in
To my brain like I was in a coma
To this day if I calculate 2 into 10
I hear choruses from Oklahoma (frustrated!)

And me Hist'ry and Geography are all fucked up too!

Caesar reminds me of Oliver Twist
Ann Boleyn will always be Gigi

And the Man from La Mancha is the Knockmealdown
Mountains
And Anything Goes is the Caspian Sea! . . .

Announcement 5 (*bing*)   Apologies customers for the huge
crowd of foreign Students blocking the escalator. I
understand your frustration and I agree with those who call
them 'Piles' – They arrive in bunches, they are a pain in the
hole and they are very difficult to get rid of!

Pontius   She'll be in the lobby of the Gresham in . . . 55
minutes!! I'm sweatin with nerves! Wanna buy her
something special. I know my parents would have
worshipped her. And Fought for her. I tried to fight. By fuck
I tried. Like when I was 13. A stray ginger Tom was dead on
our carrots so Mama told me to take it to the Vulture while it
was still fresh so I did and on the way home the bees were
ticklin me pole so I tried . . . to give them attention. They
always yearned for that . . . and I fought, fighting to
Superconcentrate watching the hive. I was counting the
comings and goings in each full minute from the honey hole
in the crabapple down the end of the garden. There was
never any bother with our bees . . . The only time they
swarmed was when the Gardaí upscuttled the house on
Good Friday 2 years before looking for copies of *An Phoblacht*
and confiscated our Easter lilies!! Jesus Christ Superstar!!
You'd swear we were the Mafia of Lamont . . . Just an
ordinary republican house . . . a place of song and poems of
emancipation. Nothing else. But the swarm that day stung
the fuck out of the 4, yes, 4 cops and 2 of them passed out in
trauma. Served them right turning against their own . . .
terrorising me parents and they only proud to be Irish and
free . . . terrorising them – just gettin away with it

Lingerie 4

The Songs that are political are usually shit
But Princess Di on rollerskates would sure be a hit
Her Brutal Murder that none of the Royals will admit
Cos homicide is smashin in a Musical !!!

So if your daddy's a Warbuck or your mamma's a Mia
Move your blooming aaaarse cos you just gotta see ya
The pure imagination
The singular sensation
The price of the tickets
But how can they stick it . . .
The Ones who'd sell their baby to the Scary Child Catcher
Because they are broke or maybe even on the Scratcher
But they have to find the cash to go to London West End
And see 10 shows a weekend and fly back to tell their friends
Over Dinner of Chorizo and Fusilli with Truffles
And bore the guests to death about their Airport Kerfuffles
They're Addicted to Sondheim . . . they'll show you a funtime
In the utterly outrageous world of Musicalssss

(*Spoken*) So there's me counting the hive. Hypnotised by the
workers' waggling dance. They all knew me, and never
pricked me ever. And I was loved by them. I knew that.
Children know when they are loved. Children know more
than any adult can. It's just a simple moment in their
existence . . . everything still, perfect, pure. Mama was
packing our clothes cos the 4 of us were off to the All-Ireland
Musical Finals the next day, a Saturday and her group were
doing *The Boyfriend* and were tipped to win so Dada was
sleepin the day cos he had to do the big drive there and back
and the bees were humming and I was mappin in me head
the journey to Letterkenny . . . passin through and Carrick
and Bundoran and fuck fuck fuck fuck I got a sting on my
eyelid a bouquet of hot needles and it swelled like a
strawberry and throbbed all night so Dada said I should stay
at home and The Pelican next door would mind me for the
24 hours till they got back with ice on my face.

Vocal . . . hurt . . . Ahh Ahh Ahh x 12

Announcement 6 (*bong*)   Fridges to Freezers, Laptops to
Toasters . . . We have plug-ins and LEDs galore on the
second floor customers. You'll blow a fuse when you see our
value in the Electrical department . . . specially our half-

price vibrators but Ladies you cannot buy the big thick long
red one near the checkout . . . because that's a fire
extinguisher!!!!

FLAMES . . .

Pontius   The flames. I wasn't meant to hear the grisly stuff.
All I was told Sunday was – they were gone. Big accident and
went whoosh to Heaven. But after the Rosary I heard Holy
Helen gossipin in our kitchen repeating the Guards
describing the flames and the rigor mortis screams of Dad
like that (*freeze*) tryin to stop it all and Mam with no head and
Mercia burned beyond a crisp on the side of the road
outside Sligo and the blaze was lethal cos Dada had filled up
in Donegal and he was full up too cos they won and his flask
empty after ploughing the three of them into the wall of
Drumcliff graveyard where Yeats is buried!! Holy fuckin
Helen. A mangled heap of simmering flesh! Stop Helen will
ya Stop!

THUNDER . . .

But The Pelican was amazing . . . she was shattered poor
thing. But she organised it all. She told the Bees, turned the
mirrors to the wall, stopped the clocks and flung water out
the door every hour. She put the Trophy in Dada's grasp in
the coffin and Mama immaculate . . . still Amazonian even
lying flat . . . and they actually found her head in a field and
she laid out face heavy made up in a Charleston dress and a
Hydrangea just here, for the month that was in it. My
Mother. 'Oh you did a great job Msss Plunket' . . . said Holy
Helen and her beads clacking . . . 'Ye did a great job . . .
specially with the joined-up bits round there . . . Oh she
looks lovely and put back together . . . looks lovely!!' Well,
The Pelican exploded . . . 'She looks fuckin dead ya ignorant
bitch! And stop layvin radox bottles on your front bedwinda
pretending ya have a bathroom because ye fuckin don't and
everyone knows that your husband, yes you Mr Helen, that
you were the panties robber from all the clotheslines last
year ya fuckin perverr and ya caught sniffin them in the

confession box with the Reverend Nobber and that same
Father Nobber has been moved from parish to post all over
the country to hide him from what he did t'altar boys for
years and never arrested . . . gettin away with it . . . in a
Soutane . . . sure no wonder she always hated the church
and loved only Jesus . . . She looks lovely . . . She looks
fuckin dead ya ignorant holy bitch!!!' Mercia's casket was
talcum white. It stayed shut.

SLAM . . .

Utter darkness with a cold breeze and eerie echos . . .

Announcement 7   Many apologies customers for the
powercut I am mortified . . . so for your own safety please
stand exactly where you are and because the wifi is gone too
maybe you can chat to each other to pass the time and please
forgive the flickerings ahead till our maintenance team
fiddle with wires on the roof !!!

Number Electrics 1

In olden days the guys and dolls would dance
It was Kismet if it lasted after that
In Cabarets and Chorus lines they'd prance
With Fever on a Saturday they'd chat
When Kate got kissed on Sunday in the park
And George on 42nd Street did too
And all that jazz was glittering not dark
And Dolly said Hello and then Adieu

But now it's online in his room to find love these days
Match and Catch.com to find love
Online on that site to look for loves
And a photograph is the difference
His prettiness is the difference if he don't, or if he does

ZZZZZZZZZZZZZ

(*Spoken*) Meine Damen und Herren . . . it vas a time foor
Miracles . . . because If it vasn't for ze Pelican I would have
been sent into care. She had a letter from Mama from vay
back – giving her permission to guardian us in case of any

tragedy. (*Snap*.) I had a fantastic rearing from her. Never wanted for anything. She robbed all round her. Never caught. Put it all in her huge gob. She'd say 'Ever since I turned 16 years old I just love puttin things in me mouth!' I had the best protractors, pencils, and sharpeners in school not to mention a mountain of lego that she had stolen over a year! But most of all, I had love and company in the village. Close to others . . . (*Snap*.) Und that vas vital foor since I lost mein Parents und Mercia, ze road to mein heart vas dug up und bleeding every day.

COWS . . .

Electrics 2

Under Clery's clock excited lovers loved to meet

Instead of facebook net or mobile phones they choose to use their feet

And walking near toward the point of rendez-vous they'd wonder

If their potential wife or husband was on time thereunder

(*Spoken*) I know so many countrylads now, who live miles from any town in the hinterland. Double the number you'd think. The confident ones are fine and travel for nightclubs or a date with the odd girl. But the shy ones, hedgehog shy, are lost. And get used to being lost. And the more they're alone the isolation grows and suspicion sometimes that if they've a farm the women will gold dig and take them for every acre. Girl Judases who'd kiss any oul frog for 40 pieces of Newbridge Silver. And I must get home by 7 to milk them cows. Ever since The Vulture got sick, I'm run off me shitty oul feet . . .

Electrics 3

In happy days the Boys and Girls would smile
It was romance ever after in the end
The single ones would all be saved in time
With Tea for two or three and all be friends
But something Digital has entered left

A shop of horrors Virtual and bad
A spell of life that is of God Bereft
That devastates a Lassie and a Lad

Cos now it's online in her room to find love these days
Your husband.com to find love
Tinder on her phone to look for loves
And her Instagram is the difference
Her selfie shot is the difference if she don't, or if she does

(*Spoken, underscore of speakeazy jazzy*)   I was never an oil
painting but had a couple of girlfriends from the parish.
Short Fumbles and a sort of sex with a few. And Gillette
Lalor from Mountmellick . . . sure everyone had her,
Gillette, the best a man can get! But nothing like the Dublin
girl and I 28 old years! She was from Sutton. The northside
of Dublin but the posh part. And the teeth to prove it. Dem
days most girls had fangs and gammy gaps and the lads had
buck ones and twists. So that Hollywood grill was a rare
spectacle. Cracking girl. Felicity. I had come up for the
Leinster hurling final and got pissed in Quinn's pub in
Drumcondra with a gang of lads from Wexford, mad fuckers
but great mischief and they told me to follow them in a taxi
to the Burlington hotel nightclub and I was elephantsgerald
drunk but got in by sheer fluke cos the bouncers were too
busy throwing out this big fella and draggin him by his long
ponytail! Tina Turner there's a pale moon in the sky a one
you lay your wishes on brilliant sounds and then the Sutton
girl launched at me with Crimson lips and teeth and tits and
we ate the face off each other like a pair of rabid monsters
from the dancefloor to out the back by the hotel bins and
into a storage shed and she was savage and bit me to pieces
. . . ZZZZZZZ devoured me like . . . a filthy plague of locusts
stripped and liquefied me and drove and drove me like she
driving a bull and I loved it and it went on all night rollin
and poppin on a pile of bubble wrap that was thrown in
there. Woke up at 10 on the Monday freezing bollock naked
and she was gone but her Lemon smell of Verbena was
there. Felicity was written on a beermat and her address. I

was grinnin like a beaver on the bus back to Laois. I wrote her at the end of that week. Heard fuck all back. Ah well. At least I had enough sex to do me till my pension!!! *and how many dancers does it take to change a lightbulb???? and a 5678!!!!!*

Announcement 8   Clery's Ballroom Ladies Choice . . . Looking gorgeous flappergirls, so take your handsome lover's hand and never let it go . . . vo do dee oo!!

Charleston number . . . Chicago style then . . .

Pontius   All I really wanted was to meet a nice girl. Someone to look after me and me to do the same. So I took a chance and I went online! I hooked up with this divorcee from Portlaoise 5 year back. She was married to a prison officer. He had bate her something awful. But I gave her all my love and did fall canyon deep for her. Trusted and helped her. After 6 months poor girl got cancer . . . saw her through it – to every treatment to recovery . . . because I worshipped her. 2 years in, on me birthday she gettin dolled up but was wobbly on Bombay Sapphire and turned and boxed and battered my face with her 7 rings and tore my skin in rasher strips with her manicure and hammered me with a furnace hot curling tongs and I ran from her and didn't speak to another human for 8 months because she, for no reason, destroyed me. But I forgive her . . . don't want to lay eyes on her though. True isn't it . . . that Hurt people – hurt people!

Electrics 4

And there was trust
And there was bravery
And there was hope and prayer depending on the chance
And there was follies
And there was innocence
Because in olden days the guys and dolls, would
They'd feel the Rhythm
In Golden days the Johns and Molls would
No space between um
In better days the stags and hens would

You shudda seem um
In olden days the days the guys and dolls would dance!
And dance, dance dance danceeeeee!

ZZZZZZZZZOOOM . . . Lights back on! then Spoken . . .

A Stor . . . first found out about her . . . Summer 1994!
Member I mentioned The Pelican's Brother the Vulture
Plunket? Well he's in a home now poor oul dote but he had
trained me that year on his farm and I worked it for him and
it has kept me goin since . . . 94 and I out thinning turnips
when Frankie the postman who replaced Dada crossed the
field with a registered letter in his paw wantin a signature.
The envelope was amber like the mangles and had a blue
line down the front. To Mr Pontius Ross, Lamont, Co. Laois
. . . A girlchild was born in Dublin that month and I was her
Father. Please get in touch by post. The return address was
embossed on the posh paper. How could I forget the house
name. Gethsemane!! Jesus! The baby is very healthy and
strong. You have one month to reply. Fuckin fuck fuck!
Felicity. PS Her name is Aster and she is 8 pounds. And then
my mind projected all sorts of dead animals on me Retina
. . . creatures the Vulture would eat over the next month cos
he would cook anything he found dead on the farm from
pigeons and rabbits to any ould roadkill and cats
remember?! My mind shocked and raving.

BEES passing by!!

And that was the start of being her Father without fail. I
travelled to Dublin every Saturday morning. Felicity lived
with her parents . . . Timothy was a cooking oil importer and
worth a fortune. Yachts and Showboats all over Malahide
and Howth. Golf jumpers and breeches like a Fosset's Circus
Boo Boo but thought he was the Prince of Portmarnock.
Like his Daughter . . . he Barely looked at me. The Wife
Saskia was a total timid lady . . . never before had I seen a
woman who was the exact colour of Glass . . . and terrified of
Tim. She'd say 'Isn't that wind dreadful' or 'Can I get Nelly
in the kitchen to rustle you a bite?' Fair dues she'd always

hail me. But Felicity had no time for me at all and left notes in the hall if she had anything to say. I was allowed only 10 hours each weekend. She ran her own Beauty Salon . . . Timothy paid for it all!

Guard   Still shoppin ya Culchie!

Pontius   Ah dare ya'are Mr Security!!

Guard   One hour left and I'm off for the weekend and I am gonna get pissed out of me bollocks!!!

Pontius   Don't drive sure ya wont. I fuckin hate drink drivers.

Guard   Listen, I've been called to the office. Something mad goin' on.

FLASH . . .

Pontius   Mad is right . . . when I think of it! I meant nothing to her. Piece of shit. She'd leave me a key under the terracotta Albatross so I'd let meself in and my babygirl in her cradle just waking so I would feed her and dress her and take her out in her buggy and chat and sing to her the best I could in the park or Dollymount strand or the shops if the weather was awful and she never took her Neptune eyes off me for the whole day and her grippin me neck like a Patagonian monkey and her head the size of a coconut on me chest and her thumb in the middle of my palm and off she'd sleep and I would leave and get the last bus to Laois at half 9. So happy. Because I had my day with my dearest Daughter. But after 4 years when they stopped me seeing her . . . I lost all my reason, all belief in myself and I was in the darkest place for years, turned the pain on myself . . . blamed and bate myself, the fuckin pain . . . Fuck the ginger tom, fuck the bees for stingin me . . . fuck them for saving me, I couldn't lose the pain . . . for years . . . at all. Mama told me once . . . She told me once that on Saturn when it rains, the drops are actual diamonds . . . bone dry rain and nothing but diamonds.

Reprise of Ahh Ahh Ahh x 6 while lying down.

Announcement 9   Silk scarves and gloves . . . get ready for the autumn ahead. Maybe that's the gift for her. I know you are nervous now cos you think I'm talkin to you Pontius! And I am! And I know that the present she will love is in the accessories section and you demented from missing her and she wrenched away from ya and you in no state to stand up and fight . . . Pontius . . . stand up, and fight.

Number Scarves 1

If I was Gene
Handsome and Lean
Crewcut and Clean
I'd carry my sadness and lift up my chest and be fully a man in the sweat of the routine

If I was Gene
Boyish and Mean
Stealing the scene
I'd rally my madness and master my best and be truly an artist and paint with my feet on the screen

But I'll never have his strength, never have his grace
Never have his confidence to celebrate my face
I'll never have his poetry, never have his skill
To drag myself up from the blackness till I come out grinning and spinning all over the place

Announcement 10   And in Kitchenware, we have saucepans of guilt and Le Creuset pots of self loathing – Whisks to batter oneself and woks to stirfry your sliced up mind

If I met Gene
The Athletic Machine
It would be a dream
I'd beg him to help jump the lakes of my tears and allow all the rain wash me clean

I'd say buddy Gene
Could we be a team
Hey would you be keen
To lampshade it all and leap like gazelles to where pastures are
nothin but green

(*Spoken*) That family in Sutton scourged me. And not a soul
to understand. Specially in Laois. Cos nobody knew – told
nobody in case I would jinx her, that she would be wiped
from my blackboard like the 2 most beautiful women had
been that time under Benbulben. And now the holy oil
family nailed me to myself . . . After all of the care. All of the
bond – beyond the bond that I had built with my darling
Angel . . . all of my time and maintenance payments they
shut me out. It was her 4th birthday. And by chance on a
Saturday. So we had the day in the garden and I put her to
bed . . . eyes locked on mine, I knew . . . I was so certain that
she knew . . . from me . . . that she was loved. She nods off
. . . And by mistake . . . I did too.

BEES . . .

Announcement 11   Wake up Pontius, Mr Ross wake up. If I
wasn't peanut bald, I'd come out of this speaker and wash
your feet with my tears . . . and dry them with my hair . . .
Wake up!!

SLAM . . .

Pontius   Midnight (*sang*)!! Shit, I'd missed me bus to
Laois. I'd sneak out and get a B and B and as I did I
remembered I left my coat in the garage earlier when I
was fixing up her first bike and when I open the door I
smelt it . . . Verbena . . . lights on and there is Felicity
naked and a stocky fella with a ponytail riding her on the
ground and I froze and she screams get out get out you're
meant to be gone and ponyboy jumps up and pins me to
wall and I see his eyes like Neptune, Neptune blue and I
nearly shit myself and I couldn't speak and then Timothy
comes in pyjama'd and what's this what's this what's this

Timothy I was gettin my coat and walked into the garage
and disturbed her and her boyfriend and Timothy says
that's not her boyfriend shur that's her first cousin Rex
and I froze again. And. And.

Announcement 12   Get it out now Pontius, Don't stop,
Shoot it out now or it will bubble and fester inside ya. Get
down to the Toy Department . . . and belt up for the
ricochets . . .

Pontius   I shouldn't have, I know I shouldn't have, but I
went too far way out of order and it gurgled up from me
centre and I called Felicity a harlot a whore and a tramp the
dirtiest bitch in the country a prostitute of today and a cunt
of Gomorrah. Asked her from my Liver 'is not your cup of
Abomination now full to the brim'. Using me for 4 long years
to cover yer filthy ways. She used me Timothy and he with
his head in his hands . . . and then she came at me like a
razorblade on fire . . .

Sound of flames bursting and red light everywhere!!

Everything went Oklahoma Sunset and I saw her pick up a
garden fork and I ran to the corner for cover and followed
and she smashed it into her own face and dropped it and
screamed like a feral Medusa and the print of the prongs
diagonal now and she 'Fuuuuuuck you' and me 'no no no I
did nathin I didn't touch her, she did it herself she did it
herself' . . .

'Hey Pontius, what's goin on, It's a Musical so sing another song!

*We're beggin ya please pleasse Pontius, what's goin on, it's a fuckin
Musical so sing another song.'*

Number Toys

AWWWW . . . MEN AWWWW . . . MEN!
Men are bastards to the core – they never weep they
never feel
Don't believe a word they lie . . . that's what boys are made of!

They only want to fuck and run no room for parenting or love
For Rats and Snails and Hootenanny tails – that's what's Boys are
made of!

Barry married Suzie but they had a buckaroo
He tries to see his son when best he can
But Suzie keeps a cancelling on custody days
Says the boy is feeling dizzy or he has to have a scan
That he's Fluee or he's tuckered out with Asthmatic coffs
There's no way she'd let him out it would be mad
So she creates Calamities on Barry's days off
To make it so impossible for the Son to see his Dad
Because, Because, Because Because . . .

Chorus!! . . . .

Martin from the Prairie found out something really scary
His wife was saddlin his best friend for years
When they took it to the Judge it was she who had
the grudge
Said she want 80/20 thru her Lonestar tears
The twins now live with her and he pays maintenance each week
But she demands it to increase and that she is broke
Despite the fact that she smokes 40 Marlboro each day
And feeds the daughters just McDonald's and full fat coca coke
Because because, because because

Chorus!!!! . . . .

Red fades.

(*Spoken*) I was never Adam, or Casanova. I was always
ordinary. I was never Hamlet or Elvis. But I was Pontius . . .
the father. That was my only deep joy. And now the cops are
pulling me out of Gethsemane and she screamin look what
you did to my face and I shouting about my rights and she
says I have nothin cos I'm not on the birthcert and she
foaming at the mouth runnin at me swinging the Albatross
over her head and I says girl look at yourself look at yerself
with your Gucci bangles and your Closets full of Fendi bags
and botox fuckin mouth . . . Ye see, Felicity . . . ya can put

Chanel Lipstick on a pig – but it's still a fucking pig and A
Stor at the window as I being mashed into a van and she
screaming like an infant Aborigine being butchered by the
British empire for Daddy Daddy my Daddy and I spent the
night in, yes, a cell, covered in snot, blood and soft shit cos I
was in shock and couldn't speak with the shaking to defend
myself and she barred me from seeing A Stor.

Scarves 2

But I'll never have his stamina, never have his style
To jeté through the clouds above and land here with a smile
I'll never have his number, never be his pal
To ask him to join the fight for me and my gal
Or to go on the town with Sinatra and Debbie
And down to Havana just givin it wellie
With Cyd Charisse and Garland and you Mr Kelly
Cha cha cha and Rumba till our legs are like Jelly

(Latin American number dance break)

And I'd be Serene
At the end of the routine
Cos I would have been
In the footsteps of someone with sparkle and sheen
The pain is washed clean
Because I would have danced . . . beside Gene

(*Spoken*) No Charges. She dropped the accusation. But
through Solicitors, I begged Her. Pleaded Calmly. Could I
continue to be a part of Aster's life. Could I have any access
because of our bond. She says No. And No No No. I was
afraid to ever come to Dublin again because, I was certain if I
saw Felicity, I would . . . Honestly . . . I would have unzipped
her throat like the Demon Barber of Fleet Street. I talked to
other fathers who had been alienated. They had the same
killer desires. After a year got a date in a Family Law Court.
They granted unenforceable access at her discretion. She
won. Got all her way. Gettin away with it. Reimbursed all my
maintenance. Timothy wrote a Cheque in his sweet charity. I

fucked it in the Liffey. I almost threw myself in too. So many Fathers have done so before me, so many who couldn't take the separation – any more. No access. Socially engineered out of the picture . . . Just because I was, ordinary, not Hercules, just a man.

Announcement 13   So here in this Palace of memories, Everything most go . . . No return Policy Pontius, everything must be told. Get me some tinfoil, cardboard and some scissors . . . I'll make ya a star Pontius and take you away from all of this shit! (*Tellers cashing.*)

Pontius   Hold on! The Pelican always said that we die to make room for another . . . to make time, for another. She passed herself last month. You'd think that she would have choked years ago with all the clepto bootie, but no. She smuggled knives and forks and spoons for years from the Killeshin Hotel till she had a full canteen of cutlery. But last month . . . Alone watching *The Apprentice* on TV balmed out on her sofa and a segment of Chocolate Orange got her. [shoes on] Imagine then I caught Holy Helen in the morgue . . . fuckin cheek of her . . . puttin scarlet lipstick on the poor Pelican – shur The Pelican never wore a screed in her life – Fuckin Helen . . . so I grabbed it off her mashed it underfoot and next day in the Church I banned her from the funeral. Walked her down the fuckin Nave by the nape of her neck and near the back door we passed this Lone fella in a moss green suit kneeling and staring forward with dark wet eyes a few years younger than me and that afternoon when I came home half pissed he was on my mind like a strange puzzle but I was distracted at around 4 by a knock at the door and Frankie with a pen and I signed for a second registered letter. Go on, ya can say it now!!!

Announcement 14   Thank you Sir. Ohhh we have bandwagon value in footwear . . . (whispers) . . . So Pontius . . . be the pilot . . . take control now . . . there is the Staircase . . . you're going up, so take it . . . and dance your little ass off!!!

Number Shoes 1

I feel like Astair A Stor
And nobody felt before
The joy that entrances my feet

If Ginger was here A Stor
I'd swing her around the floor
Like Eider feathers A Stor, or a leaf

Cos if Fred was here now I would kick his white ass
I would outshine the Master with luminous class
For I've got a letter from my beautiful lass
A Stor A Stor A Stor A Stor A Stor

I'm floating on air A Stor
Dancin like a Hoor A Stor
The postman he hugged me and I cried

I'd kiss Tony Blair A Stor
I'd hump Donald Trump A Stor
If I thought it would keep this indescribable feeling I have inside

But Fred would have his Everest to conquer my high
He'd have to have a thousand legs to take off and fly
Cos I've got correspondence like no other guy from
A Stor A Stor A Stor A Stor A Stor

(*Spoken*) Mammy on Galatians 9. . .5 'For every man shall
bear his burden.' Up to last week, I was locked out of me
own life – like watching someone else's. Like I was
ghostsinging behind a screen but there was nobody
mouthing out front . . . Locked out like the workers in 1913
and Larkin outside fighting for them. All robbed of their
lives by a powerful abuse. But last week this came from me
daughter . . . Mr Pontius Ross, Lamont, Co. Laois. And she
said she was taking a chance, that she never forgot me and
that she demanded details from her mother . . .

Shoes 2

My happiness increasing by 500 per cent

Like winning euromillions it's meant to be it's meant

It's wonderful magnificent it's all Heaven sent

A Stor A Stor A Stor A Stor A Stor.

Announcement 15   But why today, why here, why now, why why why why why why why????

Pontius   She is leaving to Australia on a work visa next week for a year Hairdressing . . . and she wanted to meet me before she went because she is 21 today and wanted a fresh start and she would be at the Gresham if I wanted to meet her too and that it was a gamble but she didn't give me phone numbers or anything because if it was meant to be, it would happen. And it's about to . . .

Announcement 16   And now a sudden Closingdown Sale. Right now, Top floor, Bridalgowns and Debutantes . . . Prices are Slashed in this Fairytale event . . .

Number Gowns

I could linger on the hundreds and thousands of days
That I missed having cornflakes with you
All the pancakey Tuesdays and pancakey ways
Not a frying pan flipped nor a trip to the zoo

Never covered your schoolbooks with wallpaper sheets
Or my Breath . . . on your fingers in winter
Never fed you with soup and the softest of sweets
Not my crying girl kissed when you stood on a splinter

Both: But who gives a shit about things that we missed
All of those moments and years
Who gives a shit about memories missed
Because all that matters is here, and now
All that matters is here.

I have dreamt of this moment for 200 months
Now it's minutes before our reunion
And I haven't a clue you can call me a dunce
For I'm feeling no fear, but some sort of confusion
For all of my hate for your mother is gone

All of the bitterness all of the bile
I forgive her and wish her pure good from now on
Cos I will lay eyes on my Stor in a while

Her 'Aaaaa's the Chorus Solo then it repeats below but sung by both . . .

Both   *So who gives a shit about things that we missed*
All of those moments and years
Who gives a shit about memories missed
Because all that matters is this, and now
All that matters is here

A Stor   *The smell of your old spice was always with me*
Your market song lyrics one piggy two three
Though your face was a blur but I always could see
The beautiful smile of my Father

Like a cloud beside me
A mist around me
A Gershwin shroud of love
a certainty
that you'd
come back for me
(a Cole Porter storm protecting me)

Him   *So I just got the gift the most beautiful gift* (reveals bag)
But it's never enough for my Girl
It's wrapped up with adoring and ribbons of love
If I had enough paper I'd wrap up the world

A Stor   *So who gives a damn about moments before*
They are gone let's forget and move on
And our joy is the swell that will drown all the hell
as we're drawing together on the waves of this song

Both   *Only minutes to go to the end of before*
Next and new is all that lies ahead
May our future be crammed with incredible bliss
May the times be impeccable like the watch of the Swiss
May beyond be the limit and before we'll dismiss

Because all now that matters is here, my girl
All that now matters is here, my Dad
All that matters is here.

Guard   Take your coat ya redneck! Have to ask you
to leave.

Pontius   Closing down? Is something wrong?

Guard   Just been told to get everyone out. Safe travels
sonny boy.

Pontius   Jesus me nerves is in bits.

Announcement 17   Pontius . . . the icing on the cake will be
a card from Eason's across the road. Get her one with the
key of the door or one with Kangaroos no no get her one
with thistles and heather and tell her all about her Grandad
Morris Minor singing from Brigadoon . . . back then . . .
when you were small, when you knew from the tips of your
little boy toes that you . . . were loved.

Sounds of city, Luas, hubbub traffic lights, beeps. Car swerving.
huge beeps. Bang! Then under the following . . . Dawn . . . rural
sound like at the start birds, cows, water . . .

Pontius   I knew I seen all this before. My last minutes
flashin before me. And an Ambulance took me to the Mater
passing the Gresham where she waited for an hour and left
in a flood of grief and her gift is God knows where. A Stor
. . . I hung around you for 2 days . . . I was the fog around
your Toyota, the breeze under your number 33 door, the
tingle on your forehead . . . but I'm free now. And so happy.

BEES . . .

I flew up here to a field way up in the Welkin. A buzzy bee
loud glade. Peace dropping slow. And below 400 worker
bees were locked out of Clery's forever for the bombs of
greed were dropped the shop!

Announcement 18 *(bing bong . . . angelic)*   Safe home
Pontius. And . . . Remember, you can't bate Clery's if you're
Gable or Munroe . . .

Pontius   And there is Mercia waving and . . . well fiddly
diddly dee!!. And look. No nerves, at all. 5 o'clock this
mornin, the blackbirds called the Sun. You're the first
people to ever know that.

AHH AHH AHH x 12 . . . as lights fade . . .

The End.